VINCE CARTER

CHOOSE *YOUR* COURSE

Positively For Kids®
811 Kirkland Ave, Suite 200
Kirkland, WA 98033
www.positivelyforkids.com

Carter, Vince, 1977-
Vince Carter—Choose your Course/ by Vince Carter with Greg Brown.
48 p. : ill. (mostly col.), ports. ; 26 cm (...series...)
Summary: Describes the life of Vince Carter, basketball player for the Toronto Raptors,
and his philosophy that it's not the challenges one faces in life, but the daily choices one
makes to meet those challenges that make the difference between success and failure.
Audience: Grades 4 – 8

ISBN 0-9634650-2-3

I. Carter, Vince, 1977-. Juvenile literature. 2. Basketball players—United States—
Biography—Juvenile literature. 3. Basketball players—Canada—Biography—Juvenile
literature. [I.Carter, Vince, 1977-. 2. Basketball players—Biography.]
I. Brown, Greg, 1957-. II. Title.

796.323/092—dc21[B]

Library of Congress Control Number:
2004091869

Photo Credits:
All photos courtesy of Vince Carter and family except the following:
AP/Wide World: 26 top right; 26 bottom left; 29 left; 29 right; 35; 39 top; 43 right; 45.
Corbis: 3; 39 bottom right. *Daytona Beach News-Journal*: 14 top left; 17 left; 20. Nigel
Cook/*Daytona Beach News-Journal*: 18 right. Getty Images: 13 left; 15; 23; 24 left; 24 right;
25 left; 25 right; 42 right. Hamish Blair/Getty Images: 32 left. Darren McNamara/Getty
Images: 31. NBAE/Getty Images: 26 top left; 26 bottom right; 26 middle left; 28 left; 28
right; 39 bottom left; 40; 41; 42 left. Jamie Squire/Getty Images: 33. Ron Turenne/NBAE/
Getty Images: cover. Stan Behal/Sun Media Corp.: 6. Ernest Doroszuk/Sun Media Corp.:
36. Greg Henkenhaf/Sun Media Corp.: 37. Veronica Henri/Sun Media Corp.: 47.

Special Thanks:
Positively For Kids would like to thank the people and organizations that helped make
this book possible: Vince Carter and Michelle Carter; Ann Smith of Embassy of Hope
Foundation; Mark Steinberg and Kathy Thomas of IMG; Charles Brinkerhoff; and the
Toronto Raptors.

Book Design:
Methodologie, Inc., Seattle

Printed in Canada

VINCE CARTER

CARTER

CHOOSE YOUR COURSE

BY VINCE CARTER
WITH GREG BROWN

A POSITIVELY FOR KIDS BOOK

What's up? I'm Vince Carter.

Playing in the National Basketball Association is a dream come true for me.

When I was young, I had no idea what I wanted to do when I grew up. I tried lots of different sports and had a strong interest in music.

Early on I enjoyed basketball. I could jump higher than most kids, and I could handle and shoot the ball well. I had no idea I'd grow to be 6-foot-6, 225 pounds. When I entered high school in the ninth grade I measured just 5-7. I grew 4 inches in one year.

I first started playing team basketball at the age of 7. Like most kids, I dreamed of playing in the NBA. My first goal was to play well in high school and then play college basketball. "That's great, but you better have a backup plan," my parents said. "You never know what might happen."

Some say playing in the NBA was my destiny. With my 44-inch vertical jump, maybe it was meant to be. Or maybe my hard work and my dedication paid off. Either way, I set a course and made the right choices to arrive.

YEAR **2003**

YEAR **1987**

Port Orange

Staying in the NBA is also rewarding, especially after back-to-back years with injuries to both knees and an ankle. Insane dunks were my trademark the first several years of my career. A knee surgery in 2002 gave me a scare. I didn't worry about high-flying jams anymore. I worried if I would ever walk normally again.

I've heard praise and people have screamed for my autograph. I've also heard the sting of criticism after tough losses, and second-guessing for some choices I've made.

No matter who you are, you will have good days and bad, victories and defeats, gains and setbacks. Nobody's perfect. And you can be sure that no matter how well you plan, unexpected events will happen.

The important thing is how you react to life's challenges. The daily choices you make today set a path that determines where you go and who you become tomorrow.

Just one bad choice can mess up your whole life.

> I'm about 5 years old in this picture.

> Chris and I in one of our first pictures together.

My brother, Chris, grew up in the same house as me with the same opportunities, yet he's been in jail five times because of the wrong choices he's made. It's tough to stay on the right course, and everyone has personal challenges to face. Life's rougher on some than others. I don't know why.

What I do know is this: In a basketball game, where you grew up, how much money you make, and your skin color don't count in the scorebook.

Winning is about preparation before the game and performance on the court. It's about making more good decisions than bad ones.

I think that holds true in the real world as well.

I've written this book to share with you the true stories of my life.

I'll tell you about some of my best decisions and some of my worst.

My hope is that this book will help you think about the decisions you'll make and understand that you do have the power to chart your future, starting today!

One choice nobody has is where you enter this world. You can't take credit or blame for your parents, where you were born, or your neighborhood. You get what you get.

I was fortunate to be born to two parents who loved me. They named me Vincent Lamar Carter.

My natural father loved basketball. My first day home from the hospital my father and his brother stood at my crib and passed a basketball back and forth. They put a tiny sponge basketball in my hands as soon as I could sit up.

My only brother, Chris, was born three years later, and we lived in Daytona Beach, Florida.

Basketball came naturally to me. Mom remembers taking us to the mall. As I walked, I pretended to bounce an invisible basketball. By age 5, I could dribble without looking at the ball, and I could bounce it between my legs.

I didn't have any real worries as a kid, except running across my biggest fear—snakes.

WE'VE HAD SNAKES IN OUR GARAGE AND UNDER CARS. ONE DAY I HEARD ONE IN OUR LIVING ROOM. "WE HAVE TO MOVE!" I SAID AFTER THE SNAKE WAS CAUGHT. OH MAN, I COULDN'T SLEEP THAT NIGHT. I WILL RUN AWAY FROM SNAKES EVERY TIME.

Daytona Beach, Florida

One thing I couldn't run from was the crumbling of my parents' marriage.

Mom and Dad divorced when I was 7, and I haven't had much contact with my dad since. My nature is to be a peacekeeper. When playing with friends, I'd let them have their way to avoid trouble. But I couldn't keep the peace in our house. It was the ugliest thing for me just being a young kid and experiencing that. I just knew there was a reason for it. It was a tough time.

ALMOST HALF OF ALL FAMILIES GO THROUGH DIVORCE. AS A CHILD, YOU HAVE NO CHOICE IN THE MATTER. IT'S IMPORTANT TO REALIZE THE DIVORCE IS NOT YOUR FAULT. THE ONLY THING YOU CAN DO IS KEEP A POSITIVE ATTITUDE AND HAVE HOPE THINGS WILL WORK OUT. CHRIS AND I LIVED WITH MOM. IT WAS COOL. WE MADE NEW FRIENDS. CHRIS AND I SURVIVED THE TRANSITION JUST FINE.

> The 1986 explosion of the Challenger is burned into my memory.

> During elementary school I became the captain of the safety patrol.

A few years later, two days after my ninth birthday, I witnessed true hardship on January 28, 1986.

Living just 60 miles from Cape Canaveral gave us front-row seats for all the space shuttle launches.

I vividly remember sitting at South Daytona Elementary School watching the Challenger Space Shuttle race towards the stars. All of a sudden it was like the sun exploded in the brilliant-blue sky. Boom! A fuel leak created a terrible fireball, killing all seven crew members, including Christa McAuliffe, the first teacher in space. Everyone was stunned. It was unbelievable. I didn't understand what happened.

About a year later renewed hope grew in our family as Mom married Harry Robinson, the band director at Campbell Junior High School, where she worked as a teacher.

We moved to Tomoka Oaks, a mostly white, upper middle class neighborhood in Ormond Beach.

I eventually called Harry my dad. He became my role model and taught me many things. Chris and I immediately showed our athletic gifts in the neighborhood. We played lots of sports. Mom's rule was we had to do our homework first before playing outside.

I enjoyed trying new things. My attitude was I might not be the best, but I'm going to give it my best try. Mom always encouraged us to try different things, saying, "You never know, you might discover you have a hidden talent."

At various ages, I played soccer, football, tennis, basketball, volleyball, ran track, and competed in the high jump. I never devoted all my energies, 24/7, to basketball. It would have burned me out. I had many interests. I also became an avid videogame player and decent skateboarder.

Skating on ice, however, wasn't my thing. In sixth grade, a band trip to Six Flags in Atlanta, Georgia, became an embarrassing memory.

We all went ice skating. Most kids hugged the wall as they circled the rink. I decided to skate to the middle to show off. I took it slow and wobbled out to where everyone could see me. Then I lost my balance and fell face first on the ice.

> The four picture slides: spiking a volleyball in high school, Chris and I in our Sunday best, Harry at work, and ready to play soccer.

> Below is our family portrait with Harry.

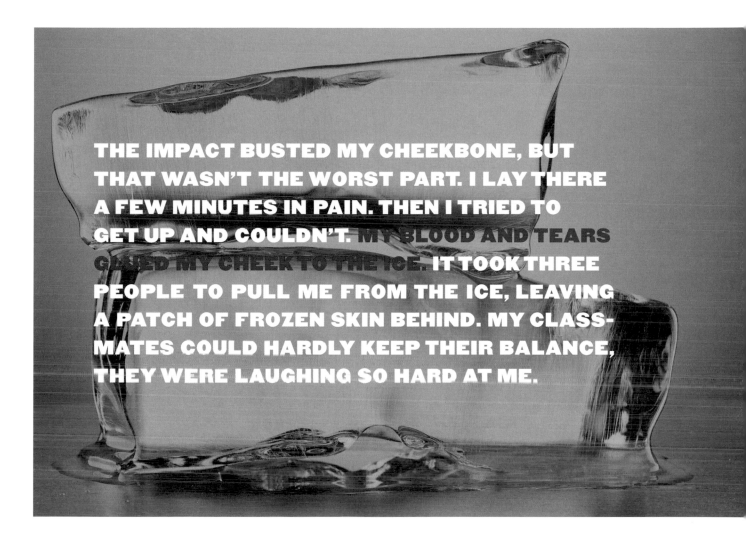

THE IMPACT BUSTED MY CHEEKBONE, BUT THAT WASN'T THE WORST PART. I LAY THERE A FEW MINUTES IN PAIN. THEN I TRIED TO GET UP AND COULDN'T. MY BLOOD AND TEARS GLUED MY CHEEK TO THE ICE. IT TOOK THREE PEOPLE TO PULL ME FROM THE ICE, LEAVING A PATCH OF FROZEN SKIN BEHIND. MY CLASS-MATES COULD HARDLY KEEP THEIR BALANCE, THEY WERE LAUGHING SO HARD AT ME.

Another thing kids teased me about in school was my glasses. I got glasses my sophomore year in high school.

Until then, I didn't know how blind I was. I couldn't see things far away, which is called being nearsighted. The doctor wondered, "How could you see the rim when you played basketball?"

The rim appeared blurry when I played before, but that was normal to me. Plus I knew what to do when I got close to the basket. If your vision is blurry or you get tired quickly reading, maybe you need glasses, too.

When I got my glasses, everything became bright and clear. I couldn't believe it.

What people tease me about these days are pictures of when I was a drum major in high school. I was the leader of our marching band my senior year. It's a big honor. Being in the band isn't always seen as the cool thing to do. In the South, band competitions are a big deal and the challenge is intense. I love music, and I loved being in the band.

MY STEPDAD'S GIFT TO ME WAS SHARING HIS LOVE OF MUSIC. WE'D GO TO HIGH SCHOOL FOOTBALL GAMES JUST TO HEAR THE BANDS PERFORM AT HALFTIME. HARRY HAD AN AMAZING EAR. OUT OF 200 BAND MEMBERS PLAYING, HE COULD HEAR THE ONE PERSON PLAYING THE WRONG NOTE.

After a few years of listening, I started hearing the off-key notes, too.

Harry encouraged me to play an instrument. I started with the saxophone in fifth grade. By high school, I wanted to choose a different direction. I switched from a reed to a wind instrument—the baritone. Musically, this is quite an unusual switch. I probably could have been a quarterback in high school, but I wanted to be in the marching band. I also played in a jazz band.

I put in seven years in the band from junior high to high school. Harry, who got a job at Mainland High and became the band director, picked me to be the drum major my senior year. Undertones of jealousy could be heard. But I won people over. It taught me many things about leadership and responsibility.

Harry thought it tacky for marching bands to use sheet music on the field. Everyone had to memorize the music. So everyone counted on me to keep the beat.

> Here I am in high school. Even though I was skinny, I could block shots. I averaged 3.25 blocks a game my senior year.

I didn't miss a beat on the court, either. I first dunked the basketball in sixth grade.

I perfected the skill with practice. I'd try it every day. I messed around jamming tennis balls and volleyballs. I graduated to dunking with one leg.

I had natural jumping ability, but I trained my mind to believe it was possible.

I developed a flair for the dramatic. By my junior season in high school, our team became a fan attraction.

Frenetic fans packed our old gym for our games. So many wanted to watch, the school opened the cafeteria and broadcast home games via closed-circuit TV. We reached the semifinals of the state basketball playoffs in 1994 and lost by 5 points to Boyd Anderson High School. When you get to the main stage and lose, it's devastating.

FUN FACT >>> VINCE AVERAGED 18.8 POINTS PER GAME AND 7.6 REBOUNDS PER GAME AS A SOPHOMORE AT MAINLAND HIGH. THAT IMPROVED TO 25.4 POINTS AND 11 REBOUNDS AS A JUNIOR AND DIPPED TO 20 POINTS AND 10.5 REBOUNDS AS A SENIOR.

THE NEXT DAY I STARTED WORKING OUT FOR THE NEXT SEASON. I STARTED SAYING, "WE'RE GOING TO WIN IT ALL NEXT YEAR!"

After hearing me say it, a few others repeated it. Soon everyone on our returning team started to believe it.

We chose to think like champions the next season. Every time we stepped on the court, we treated it as a championship game. We attacked.

During one game my senior year, I sprained the wrist of my shooting hand early in the contest. The injury forced me to shoot with my left hand. I scored 32 points.

In the state playoff, Mainland beat Miami High School in the semifinals, 70-67. We advanced to the state finals and beat Fort Lauderdale Dillard, 62-45. I had 22 points, 16 rebounds, and 10 blocks. The title was our school's second state basketball championship—the Buccaneers' first was in 1939. It was a dream come true for me and it was a relief for my mom. She feared I'd have a mental breakdown if we lost because I invested so much emotionally into winning a state title.

> **Celebrating our state victory.**

> **I was honored to play in the McDonald's All American tournament.**

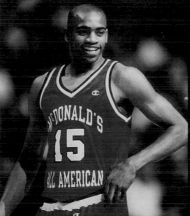

In my final two years, Mainland posted a 64-4 record with two losses a year. Mainland has won two more state boys' basketball titles since I left.

AFTER RECEIVING 76 SCHOLARSHIP OFFERS, I ACCEPTED A BASKETBALL SCHOLARSHIP TO THE UNIVERSITY OF NORTH CAROLINA. THE DECIDING FACTORS WERE THE GREAT BASKET-BALL TRADITION AND THAT THE DISTANCE WASN'T TOO FAR FOR MY FAMILY TO DRIVE TO GAMES. OF COURSE MY PARENTS WERE PROUD THE DAY I SIGNED MY LETTER OF INTENT TO PLAY FOR THE TAR HEELS.

That day I signed a contract with my mom as well. I promised to get my college degree. Mom said basketball is great, but you never know what will happen.

While the spotlight of attention was on me, my brother Chris, a freshman, seemed to become lost in the darkness of my shadow.

FUN FACT >>> VINCE RECEIVED A MUSIC SCHOLARSHIP OFFER TO BETHUNE-COOKMAN COLLEGE.

People expected him to "be like Vince." He couldn't. He struggled to find his own identity. He didn't want to be Vince's brother. He chose to go about it the wrong way.

He gave up on sports and hung out with the wrong crowd. Sometimes he'd go to class high on drugs.

My parents punished him. They took things away and grounded him. But when a person is determined to take the wrong course, only God can stop them.

One high school decision I'm proud about is I never chose the path of drugs.

I never drank alcohol during my high school and college days. To this day I've never tried weed or any other illegal drugs. I just stayed away from that stuff. I wouldn't put myself in those situations. My friends knew my stance, and I never felt any peer pressure at all.

I always wanted to stay in control. I've seen people out of control, drunk out of their minds, and they do not make good choices.

The world can be dangerous, especially when you're drunk or high.

Another time I decided not to follow the crowd came on senior skip day. Many seniors decided to miss class and go hang out at the beach.

Everyone knew my stepdad worked at the school. If I skipped school, I would have missed my dad's class. So I told my friends, "I'm not going to do it. I'll catch you later."

I wanted to go, but I saw the bigger picture. I didn't want to embarrass my parents.

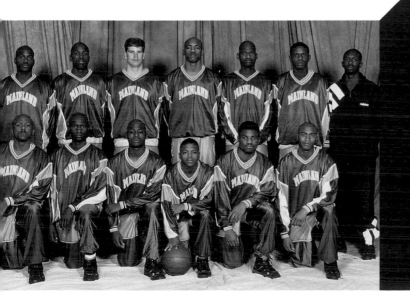

WHY DID VINCE'S SCORING STATS DROP HIS SENIOR YEAR?

He knew he had a scholarship, so he looked to feed teammates with assists so they could pad their stats in hopes they would get noticed by college coaches, too.

"Vince's stats in high school could have gone through the roof his senior year," Mainland coach Charlie Brinkerhoff said. "He was totally unselfish that way."

My freshman year in college proved frustrating. Even though I earned a starting spot on the team, I didn't play as much as I had hoped and wasn't allowed to play "my game" in legendary coach Dean Smith's structured offense.

THE TEAM'S STYLE REVEALED A WEAKNESS IN MY GAME. I NEEDED TO IMPROVE MY OUTSIDE SHOOTING. THAT SUMMER I CHOSE TO TURN FRUSTRATION INTO MOTIVATION. I WORKED HARD AND MY JUMP SHOT IMPROVED. IN MY SOPHOMORE YEAR, WE TOOK A 16-GAME WINNING STREAK INTO THE 1997 FINAL FOUR.

Arizona knocked us out in the semifinals. Teammates had to pick me up off the court because I couldn't believe we lost.

My junior year we reached the Final Four again, only to be ousted by Utah in the semifinals. Immediately after our loss, teammate Antawn Jamison, the NCAA Player of the Year, announced he'd go into the NBA draft.

I wanted to leave college a year early and join the NBA as well. But I had to convince my mom first. I told her she could rip up that contract we signed because I gave her my word I'd get my college degree. I promised to come back for summer school to finish.

 FUN FACT >>> VINCE AVERAGED 7.5 POINTS IN 31 GAMES AS A FRESHMAN AND 13 POINTS A GAME AS A SOPHOMORE. HE IMPROVED HIS SCORING AVERAGE TO 15.6 POINTS AS A JUNIOR AND WAS SELECTED FIRST-TEAM ALL-ACC.

So we made a list of the pros and cons of coming out early. Then we wrote down what could go wrong. I talked to people I trusted, current and former pro players, coaches, and scouts—not to give me the right answer, but to point me in the right direction. Coach Smith, who retired after my sophomore year, told me he thought I was ready for the NBA. I appreciated his encouragement and honesty.

After all that I decided to put my name in the 1998 NBA draft. The Toronto Raptors picked Jamison, my teammate, with their fourth pick and the Golden State Warriors took me fifth. Then the two teams immediately swapped Jamison and me.

The quick trade surprised many people, including my family. We didn't mind, though. I was excited to be chosen and thrilled to join my cousin, Tracy McGrady—T-Mac.

Kids always ask what was the first thing I bought after I signed my multimillion-dollar contract with the Raptors. Was it a hot car? A new mansion? Gold jewelry?

No, it was none of those. The first thing I invested my money in was a new foundation. I started the Embassy of Hope Foundation in my hometown. It was important for me to share my good fortune with those who are not so fortunate.

> Celebrating an ACC Tournament victory.

> Tar Heel teammate Antawn Jamison (right) and I switch hats moments after NBA commissioner David Stern (middle) announces a draft-day trade between Golden State and Toronto.

Since my rookie year, the foundation has teamed with many sponsors and raised more than $585,000 dollars for programs to support kids and families in Daytona Beach and Toronto. We strive to encourage people to believe in their dreams. Once you have hope, anything is possible.

IF EVERY CHOICE YOU MAKE IS ONLY ABOUT YOURSELF AND MONEY, THEN YOU'RE MISSING OUT ON THE REWARDS OF HELPING OTHERS. A GREAT ASSIST IS AS MUCH FUN AS SCORING IN BASKETBALL. GIVING SOMEONE AN ASSIST IN LIFE MAKES YOU FEEL LIKE A WINNER EVERY TIME.

FUN FACT >>> VINCE SOMETIMES PUTS HIS HANDS OVER HIS HEAD WITH FINGERS POINTING UP AFTER A GREAT PLAY. IT'S HIS WAY OF GIVING HIS FRATERNITY BROTHERS A SHOUT OUT. VINCE BELONGS TO OMEGA PSI PHI FRATERNITY.

25

Raptor coach Butch Carter (no relation to me) made me feel like a winner from the first day. He pushed me to step up and show the league what I could do. He had faith in me.

The first season I made the All-Rookie Team. In my second year I was voted to the All-Star Game. I was honored to be invited to the 2000 Slam Dunk Contest.

I had a little problem getting to the dunk competition. The NBA ran out of stretch limos to take long-body players from the hotel to the arena. I didn't have a ride. So the NBA got us a four-door sedan and Tracy and I squeezed into this tiny car.

As a kid I taped the Dunk Contest and studied it like an art form. I wanted to show what I could do.

MY OPENING DUNK—A BASELINE WINDMILL JAM—GOT THE FANS EXCITED. A STRAIGHT-ON JAM JUMPING FROM THE FREE-THROW LINE PUMPED UP THE HOUSE. THEN TRACY JOINED THE ACT BY BOUNCING THE BALL IN FRONT OF ME. I CAUGHT IT IN MID-AIR, SCOOPED IT BETWEEN MY LEGS AND SLAMMED IT HOME. A REVERSE 360 WINDMILL GAVE ME A PERFECT SCORE WITH ONE MORE TO GO. FOR MY FINAL TRY, I WANTED TO PUT SOME PIZZAZZ INTO IT AND BLOW PEOPLE'S MINDS.

So I jumped extra high and rammed the ball and my hand through the rim into the net up to my elbow and then hung there for a few seconds. I took home the dunk title and much more.

The Dunk Contest became my coming-out party. Suddenly it seemed everyone knew me after that.

FUN FACT >>> VINCE WAS THE ONLY ROOKIE TO LEAD HIS TEAM IN SCORING DURING THE 1998-1999 NBA SEASON. VINCE WAS ONCE FEATURED ON ESPN'S PLAYS OF THE WEEK SIX CONSECUTIVE WEEKS FOR HIS INCREDIBLE DUNKS.

27

IN THE SECOND HALF OF THAT SEASON, T-MAC AND I BECAME A FORCE ON THE COURT AND CLOSE FRIENDS OFF IT. THAT WAS SPECIAL BECAUSE WE DIDN'T GROW UP KNOWING EACH OTHER.

Together we helped lead Toronto to its first playoff appearance. In the first round, unfortunately, we lost to the New York Knicks.

We lost five games by 7 points in the series. I didn't shoot well. Many critics pointed their fingers and blamed me for the losses. It didn't bother me. I choose not to listen. I don't let negativity bring me down.

Before the next season, I learned my agent, Tank Black, lost $200,000 of my money on bad investments. He "lost" other athletes' money as well and eventually landed in jail.

That was tough to swallow. My family trusted him with everything.

You earn trust by the choices you make. It only takes one bad decision to break the bond of trust.

Tracy and I had our trust tested after the 2000 season.

The first-round playoff loss to the Knicks brought change. Coach Carter was fired and Tracy left as a free agent, signing with Orlando.

I pictured us playing together many years. But Tracy wanted his own course. I heard rumors that he grew jealous of my popularity.

We didn't speak to each other for six months. Finally, we decided we were too tight to continue this family feud. We chose to forgive.

I forgave him for leaving. You can't pick other people's paths for them. It was his choice to make. And for whatever he said or didn't say, it's history.

> Mom gives me a kiss after I won the NBA Rookie of the Year award.

> Tracy and I hug and make up after six months of not talking to each other.

That summer when Tracy left, I learned Chris, my brother, was in jail for drug possession. Chris dropped out of high school and lost his way.

The 2000 Olympics in Sydney, Australia, became my escape from frustrations. I joined the USA basketball team with a head of hair and new aggressive attitude. I had been bald since the IIth grade in high school.

THE OPENING CEREMONIES WERE UNFORGETTABLE. YOU REALIZE IT'S NOT THE RAPTORS VS. THE LAKERS. IT'S THE U.S.A. VS. THE WORLD. THE MAGNITUDE OF THE EVENT HITS YOU.

Our group of NBA players was Dream Team III. For many years Olympic rules didn't allow professional players to compete. Then at the 1992 Games in Barcelona, Spain, the first group of pro basketball players competed. The USA team included stars Michael Jordan, Magic Johnson, and Larry Bird. They were called the Dream Team. The second Dream Team won gold in Atlanta in 1996.

So the U.S. had won the last two Olympic men's basketball titles. We weren't going to let the winning streak stop with us.

The world wanted to knock us down. It was a tough tournament. We played several tight games, beating Lithuania by just 2 points in the semifinals and leading by only 4 with four minutes to go in the championship game against France.

The most talked-about play of the tournament came in the early rounds against France. I had an unbelievable dunk over the 7-2 Frenchman, Frederic Weis. People still say that it was the most amazing dunk ever.

After I missed a shot, I got the rebound and attacked the basket. Weis stood between the rim and me. I jumped right over him. I thought he slipped and fell while it happened, but he didn't. When I saw the tape, I couldn't believe it myself.

Throughout the tournament our team was criticized for perceived unsportsmanlike behavior. Some wrote I behaved badly.

Do I regret some choices I made on the world stage? I think our emotions got the best of us. We were pumping up ourselves and our teammates more than trying to put down or bully others.

SPORTS BRING OUT INTENSE FEELINGS SOMETIMES AND MY RAW EMOTIONS CAME OUT. I HAD A FEW BAD DAYS. I LET ANGER TAKE CONTROL WHEN A COUPLE OF PEOPLE TRIED TO HURT ME WITH DIRTY PLAYS. THE WORLD SAW A DIFFERENT VINCE CARTER AND DIDN'T KNOW WHAT TO THINK.

> Australian Andrew Gaze and I tangle during the Olympics.

> Winning the gold medal brought a tear to my eye when I saw my mom afterward.

> **All smiles with Olympic teammates Tim Hardaway (behind) and Kevin Garnett (right).**

To me, winning a gold medal at the Olympics is better than winning an NBA title. You get a chance to win in the NBA each year. The Olympic Games come around once every four years.

My mom wanted that gold medal for me more than I did. After we beat France 85-75, seeing Mom there for this event made me break down and cry.

The Raptors climbed higher in the 2001 playoffs as we finally got past the Knicks in the first round.

That created a showdown with Allen Iverson, the 76ers' high-scoring guard. Back and forth the momentum swung. The series went to a dramatic seventh game, the winner to the Eastern Conference finals.

The game fell on an important date for me—May 20, 2001, graduation day at the University of North Carolina. By attending summer classes, I earned my Bachelor of Arts degree in African-American studies. I kept my promise to Mom.

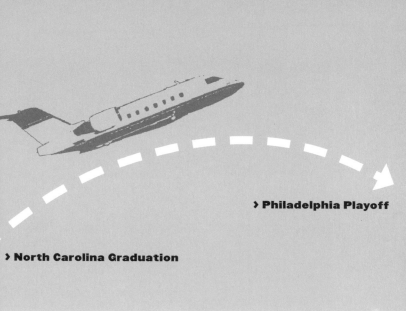

> **North Carolina Graduation**

> **Philadelphia Playoff**

Now the biggest game of my life landed on the happiest day of my education.

My decision didn't take long. I chose both. After graduation ceremonies in the morning at Chapel Hill, North Carolina, a private jet got me back to Philadelphia in plenty of time for the game. The flight took about an hour.

Our classic series ended with a classic finish. Down by one with 2 seconds to play, we called time out. I told Coach Lenny Wilkens I'd get open.

I got the ball near the sidelines beyond 3-point range and put up an off-balance shot with a defender in my face.

It rimmed out. Philadelphia won.

Some Raptor fans and some in the media questioned whether I should have gone to the graduation. Some thought it cost us the game.

I DON'T THINK SO. WHETHER I WENT TO GRADUATION OR SAT IN OUR HOTEL THAT MORNING DIDN'T MAKE A DIFFERENCE IN THE GAME. DOING BOTH DID MAKE A DIFFERENCE. I THINK IT CAUGHT KIDS' ATTENTION.

VINCE CARTER BASKETBALL ACADEMY

"Where athletes learn the game of basketball and how to be good students."

Every year since 1998 I have put on a summer basketball camp for kids. It mixes basketball and academics. After that Game 7 against Philly, the questions kids asked me changed.

Kids used to ask, "What's it like to play against Allen Iverson?"

Then they started asking, "How did it feel to graduate before Game 7?"

At the Vince Carter Basketball Academy, athletes learn the game and how to be students. There is time to play and time to go into the classroom. They learn computer skills, such as how to find information for a book report or how to find a career. We've had some great athletes who couldn't read. Teachers and parents coddle these guys because they are good athletes.

What that does, however, is hurt the athlete in the end by limiting career choices after sports.

EARNING MY COLLEGE DEGREE IS PROBABLY THE MOST IMPORTANT THING THAT I'VE ACCOMPLISHED SO FAR IN MY LIFE.

The reason I say that is because I was able to keep my promise to my family, and I got the chance to be a regular person in achieving my goal.

I'm very proud of my brother for having the courage to go back to school and earn his high school diploma. While I don't agree with all his choices, he'll always be my brother. I'll always love him, and I'll do whatever I can for him.

The thing about getting your education, whether it's finishing high school, learning a trade, or getting a college degree, it's a sure thing. If you do the work —go to class and pass—you'll get it. And you'll always have it.

In sports, you can work your whole life for a goal of becoming a professional or winning a championship and there is no guarantee it will happen. A twist, a break, a fall can end it all.

No athlete wants to think about getting hurt. My biggest fear is being under-cut (having someone knock me off balance while in the air). Because I broke my wrist by being hit in the legs while in flight, that's been my nightmare ever since high school. But I don't let that change my game. You don't have time to worry about your fears during competition.

The scariest sound an athlete can hear is a pop inside your body. When you hear that snap, you know something bad has happened.

I've heard it too many times.

Our promising 2001-02 season found me watching 22 of 82 games from the bench. I went up for a dunk in San Antonio and my legs tangled with Tim Duncan.

I LANDED AWKWARDLY, INJURING MY LEFT KNEE. I HOBBLED AROUND BEFORE FINALLY UNDERGOING A KNEE OPERATION IN MARCH, ENDING MY SEASON.

I cheered on my teammates as they staged a late-season rally, winning 12 of 14 games, including a team record nine straight, to make the playoffs without me.

The first few weeks of the 2002-03 season found me injured again. This time chronic pain in my left kneecap put me out for 10 games.

A few weeks after my return, I heard a pop in my right knee during practice and sat out 23 games. My season ended six games early with an ankle sprain. All together I sat out almost half the season, missing 39 of 82 regular-season games.

That season I received some criticism at the 2003 All-Star Game. This was Michael Jordan's final All-Star game but he had not been voted by the fans as a starter. The buzz that weekend centered around who would give up their starting spot for Michael. I told All-Star coach Isiah Thomas on Saturday that I would give Michael my starting spot. But I kept it a secret from everyone else. During the game introductions, I grabbed Michael's arm and slung him onto the court to take my position. Some people thought I waited too long to make my decision, but I had it planned all along.

FUN FACT >>> VINCE SURPASSED DOUG CHRISTIE (4,448) ON MARCH 2, 2001, AGAINST NEW JERSEY TO BECOME THE RAPTORS' ALL-TIME LEADING SCORER.

Back-to-back years with serious injuries tested me. However flustered fans get, or Toronto's management feels, I'm the most frustrated of all. I'm not a dunking machine. The pain of sitting out is real. I've felt like the forgotten soul.

I've heard all the complaints—I'm overrated. I'm fragile. I'm not a leader. I'm not aggressive enough. I'm not scoring enough.

It's hard to hear people say those things. But I accept that it comes with the territory. You take the sour with the sweet. To me it's not about my stats, sports is about winning. Every day I'm committed to doing what I can to help our team win.

The spring and summer of 2003 I did something I haven't done in many years. I let my body rest. I took some time off and let my body heal. It made all the difference. When a spot opened on the USA Olympic Qualifying Team, I was ready to play like the Vince Carter of old.

I began the 2003-2004 season confident and excited to prove I was healthy and ready to play. I got off to a solid start, including a 43-point game in November (my NBA career high is 51 points).

MIDWAY INTO THE SEASON I WAS BACK TO SCORING 20-PLUS POINTS A GAME. FANS VOTED ME A STARTING SPOT IN THE 2004 ALL-STAR GAME IN LOS ANGELES. IN THE GAME, IVERSON FED ME THREE TIMES FOR SATISFYING DUNKS AS I SCORED 11 POINTS. I FINALLY FELT BACK ON COURSE.

> My fiancee Ellen Rucker and me.

Where will my course lead? I have many goals still on my to-do list—an NBA Championship, League MVP, All-Star MVP, All-NBA Defensive First Team. I have a long way to go, so I have plenty to keep me motivated on the court.

Off the court, I've found someone I love and have asked Ellen Rucker to marry me. She's a doctor from South Carolina. We met at the University of North Carolina at Chapel Hill where she was a cheerleader. So I look forward to our life together.

I will continue my charity work through the Embassy of Hope and other organizations. I plan to get my master's degree in communications or business. Maybe I'll be faced with another Game 7 on graduation day. I hope so.

I believe there's an ultimate roadmap for my life, and yours. None of us knows where exactly that leads, which makes life exciting. We do have the free will to stay on course or go off-road.

The good news is there is always a way back to the right road. So my advice is to think before you act. Make decisions that will lead to the best options down the road. Exercise your mind. Stay in school, or go back to school, and earn an education or trade skill. Make choices to stay healthy. Make choices to stay in control.

In the end, it's up to you to choose your course.

NBA Career Averages

In 310 games, Vince averaged

24.1	points
5.4	rebounds
3.7	assists
1.36	steals
1.08	blocks
37.8	minutes

Career Highs

Points	51	vs. Phoenix 2/27/00
Field Goals Made	20	vs. Milwaukee 1/14/00
Field Goals Attempted	36	@ Philadelphia 1/21/01
Three-Point Field Goals Made	8	@ Utah 11/10/01
Three-Point Field Goals Attempted	14	@ Utah 11/10/01
Free Throws Made	22	@ Phoenix 12/30/00
Free Throws Attempted	27	@ Phoenix 12/30/00
Offensive Rebounds	7	2 Times
Defensive Rebounds	13	@ Houston 3/24/04
Total Rebounds	15	2 Times
Assists	12	2 Times
Steals	6	2 Times
Blocks	6	vs. Chicago 3/28/99
Minutes Played	63	vs. Sacramento 2/23/01

as of March 31, 2004

VINCE'S LIFETIME STATS

	GP	FGMA	Pct	3FGM-A	Pct	FTM-A	Pct	Reb	Avg	A	TO	B	S	Pts	Avg
Mainland High School															
'92-93	27	125-228	55	60-146	41	76-102	75	206	7.63	52	–	58	40	506	18.7
'93-94	32	227-377	60	70-188	37	149-194	77	354	11.06	92	–	91	30	813	25.4
'94-95	34	226-376	60	50-147	34	118-185	64	377	10.47	149	–	117	83	720	20.0

	GP	FGMA	Pct	3FGM-A	Pct	FTM-A	Pct	Reb	Avg	A	TO	B	S	Pts	Avg
North Carolina Tar Heels															
'95-96	31	91-185	49.2	19-55	34.5	31-45	68.9	119	3.8	40	36	16	20	232	7.5
'96-97	34	166-316	52.5	36-107	33.6	75-100	75	152	4.5	63	47	26	29	443	13.0
'97-98	38	224-379	59.1	44-107	41.1	100-147	68	195	5.1	74	40	36	45	592	15.6
Totals	103	481-880	54.7	99-269	36.8	206-292	70.5	466	4.5	197	123	80	114	1267	12.3

	G	GS	MPG	FG%	3P%	FT%	Rebounds Per Game			APG	SPG	BPG	TO	PF	PPG
							OFF	DEF	RPG						
Toronto Raptors Career Averages															
'98-99	50	49	35.2	.450	.288	.761	1.90	3.80	5.70	3.0	1.10	1.54	2.20	2.80	18.3
'99-00	82	82	38.1	.465	.403	.791	1.80	4.00	5.80	3.9	1.34	1.12	2.17	3.20	25.7
'00-01	75	75	39.7	.460	.408	.765	2.30	3.20	5.50	3.9	1.52	1.09	2.23	2.70	27.6
'01-02	60	60	39.8	.428	.387	.798	2.30	2.90	5.20	4.0	1.57	.72	2.57	3.20	24.7
'02-03	43	42	34.2	.467	.344	.806	1.40	3.00	4.40	3.3	1.12	.95	1.72	2.80	20.6
Playoff	15	15	43.9	.415	.366	.810	3.10	3.30	6.40	5.0	1.53	1.60	2.33	3.80	25.7
All-Star	4	3	23.3	.489	.300	1.000	1.30	1.30	2.50	2.0	1.25	.25	2.00	.80	12.0

www.vincecarter15.com

> Vince has donated $2.5 million of his own money to fund an athletic center at Mainland High School.

EMBASSY OF HOPE
A VINCE CARTER FOUNDATION

Vince established the Embassy of Hope, a non-profit foundation, in 1998 to help address the needs of children and their parents.

The foundation's slogan, "Believing in Your Dreams," represents Vince's lifelong commitment to perseverance and achievement—qualities that have enabled him to excel as an athlete and as a person committed to helping those less fortunate.

The values embodied in a winning attitude are important to Vince, and he wants to share them with others. Whether it's on the court as a colorful player, in the classroom as a speaker, or one-on-one as a mentor, Vince continues to encourage children to work hard so that they, too, may have a chance to experience the same joy of accomplishment and success that he has—both on and off the court.

Since its inception, the Embassy of Hope has raised $585,000 and has touched the lives of countless children in the United States and Canada by contributing funds to more than 50 non-profit organizations. Using money raised through the foundation's annual "Vince Carter Summer Jam" weekend, the Embassy of Hope has made a difference for children in Vince's home state of Florida, in his adopted hometown of Toronto, and elsewhere, through a number of activities, including:

Providing continuous support to the Children's Home Society since 1999

Awarding six $5,000 Vince Carter Believing in Your Dreams academic scholarships since 2001

Distributing 680 food baskets for families at Thanksgiving and Christmas

Funding creation of a $130,000 pro-sized basketball court in Toronto's Dixon Park

Donating funds to Magdalene, Inc. to help establish a secure "safe" house of residence

Providing sneakers for the Wellness Program at Tomoka Correctional Institution

Supporting the Kiwanis Club of Daytona Beach for "first day of school outfit"

Donating $25,000 to Bloorview MacMillan Children's Centre for the support of kids with disabilities

Donating $25,000 for the Vince Carter room at the Ronald McDonald House in Toronto, which will be used for accommodations for the families of hospitalized seriously ill children

Giving $25,000 to Camp Jumoke, a camp for children afflicted with sickle cell anemia

Contributing $15,000 to Children's Aid Foundation for three $5,000 Vince Carter Believing in Your Dreams scholarships

Donating $75,000 to United Way of Greater Toronto

Donating funds for the construction of a new library with a children's section and auditorium in a poverty-stricken section of Daytona Beach

Sponsoring a "Believing in Your Dreams" essay contest in Vince's home county, Volusia County, Florida, for 84 children ranging in age from 9 to 18

Embassy of Hope is a Florida-based 501(c)(3) charitable organization, which is also registered with Revenue Canada. Anyone interested in assisting the Embassy of Hope Foundation may make a donation and send it to: P.O. Box 9596, Daytona Beach, FL 32120 USA. embassy1@bellsouth.net.

Index

Websites for Vince Carter

Vince Carter   www.vincecarter15.com
Toronto Raptors   www.raptors.com
NBA   www.nba.com
Toronto Sun   www.torontosun.com
ESPN Sporting News   www.espn.com
Sports Illustrated   www.si.com
Sports Illustrated for Kids   www.sikids.com
Frontier College   www.frontiercollege.org